GARDEN *of* ISLAM

OWL
AND THE
DAWN PRAYER

By
Hediyah Al-Amin

Goodword**kidz**
Helping you build a family of faith

What if a rooster—
who crowed everyday at dawn
to wake everyone for prayer—
one day didn't crow?
The creatures didn't wake
up for prayer.

But the owl was awake, because it stays up all night. So the owl woke the hen and said, "Hen, tell the rooster to crow becuase it is time for the dawn prayer."

But the hen was angry with the rooster so she would not speak. So the owl went to wake fox and said, "Fox, chase the hen, because she won't tell the rooster to crow and it's time for the dawn prayer."

But the fox was feeling lazy, so the owl went to wake wolf and said: "Wolf, devour the fox, because he won't chase the hen and the hen won't tell the rooster to crow and it's time for the dawn prayer."

9

But the wolf ate late last night so did not want to devour the fox. So the owl went to wake the farmer and said, "Farmer, capture the wolf, because he won't devour the fox and the fox won't chase the hen and the hen won't tell the rooster to crow and its time for the dawn prayer."

But the farmer was still snoring and didn't hear the owl. So the owl went to the farmer's wife and said, "Farmer's wife, sprinkle some water on your husband's face so he will wake up and capture the the wolf, because the wolf won't devour the fox and the fox won't chase the hen and the hen won't tell the rooster to crow and it's time for thc dawn prayer."

But the farmer's wife was still snoring, too. So the owl went to the baby and said, "Wake up little baby and cry so your mom will wake and sprinkle some water on your dady's face so he will wake up and capture the wolf, because the wolf won't devour the fox and the fox won't chase the hen and the hen won't tell the rooster to crow and it's time for the dawn prayer."

14

But the baby didn't understand. The owl became very sad because he didnot want anyone to miss the prayer, so he began to cry.

When the owl cried, it made the baby also cry, and therefore his mother came to pick him up.

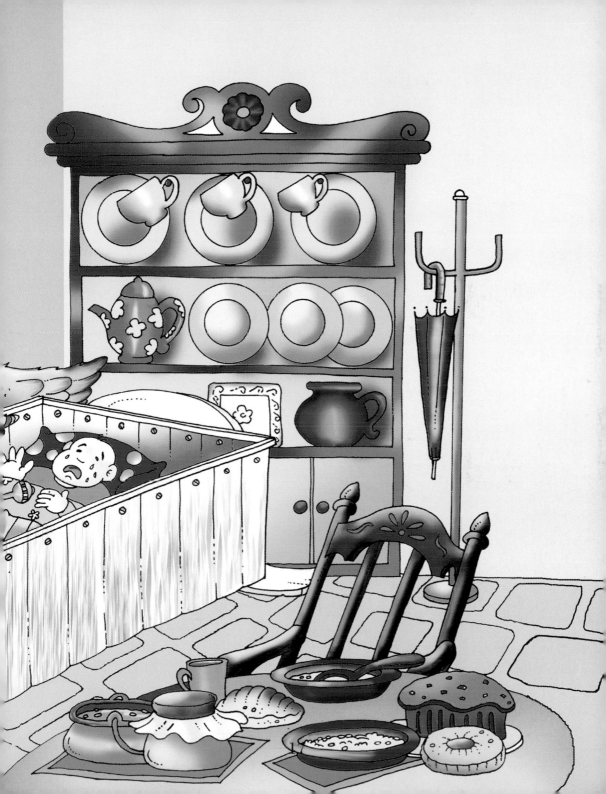

Then she sprinkled some water on the farmer's face. So the farmer woke up and then he made the call to prayer.

When the wolf heard the call, he knew that the farmer would be out to catch him soon, so the wolf went to devour the fox.

But the fox ran to chase the hen and the hen told the rooster to crow and then all creatures prayed the dawn prayer.

Comprehension Questions:

1. Why didn't creatures wake up for prayer?

2. Why didn't the hen tell rooster to crow?

3. Why didn't the fox chase the hen?

4. Was the wolf hungry?
   Why or why not?

5. What did the owl want
   the farmer's wife to do?

6. Why did the baby cry?

1. Why do Muslims pray at dawn? Can you find proof from the Quran and Sunnah that this is obligatory?

2. What did the Prophet ﷺ tell us about why roosters crow?

3. Do animals pray? Can you find proof from the Quran and Sunnah to support your answer?

4. Is it proper Islamically for a wife to sprinkle some water in her husband's face for waking him for salah? Why or why not?

Suggested Activities:

Act out the story as a skit or short play. If you have the proper materials and an imaginative mind, you can even design costumes.

Do some research about owls. Why do owls stay up all night? What other interesting facts can you find out about them?

Do you know how to make the call to prayer?

Memorize it and say it loudly in your class or at home.